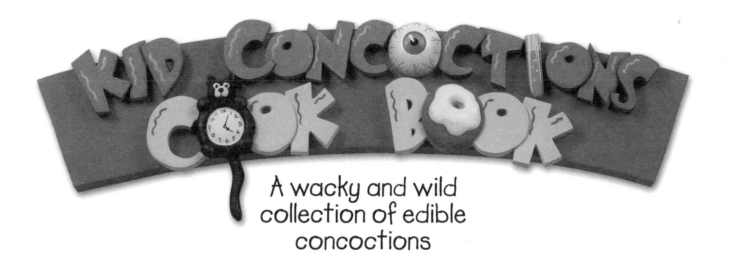

A wacky and wild
collection of edible
concoctions

JOHN E. THOMAS
DANITA THOMAS

A publication of The Kid Concoctions Company

CREDITS:

Cover art design:	Robb Durr
Cover photography:	Jack Dragga
Illustrators:	Robb Durr, Zachariah Durr
Production:	Laurence J. Nozik
Authors:	John E. Thomas & Danita Thomas
Publishing Company:	Kid Concoctions Company

ISBN: 0-9661088-4-1

Visit our website:
www.kidconcoctions.com

Email comments and questions to:
KidConcoct@aol.com

Manufactured in the Untied States of America
10   9   8   7   6   5   4   3   2   1

DEDICATION

We would like to dedicate this book
to our 4 wonderful children:

Kyle,
Kalie,
Kellen
and
Christian

"Thank you for filling our lives with
love, happiness and never ending adventures!"

ACKNOWLEDGMENTS

We would like to thank the children, parents, grandparents, educators, and all the others who have supported Kid Concoctions and helped it grow into more than we ever dreamed possible.

Other titles by John and Danita Thomas:

The Ultimate Book of Kid Concoctions (ISBN# 0966108809)

The Ultimate Book of Kid Concoctions #2 (ISBN# 0966108817)

The Ultimate Book of Holiday Kid Concoctions (ISBN# 0966108833)

Kid Concoctions & Contraptions (ISBN# 0966108884)

Kid Concoctions of Biblical Proportions (ISBN# 0805444475)

FOREWARD

Over the last ten years, the Kid Concoctions books have been a favorite of teachers and parents because they promote basic math, science and life skills, in a very entertaining format. We are thrilled to share with you the 6th book in the Kid Concoctions series, the *Kid Concoctions Cook Book*.

In the *Kid Concoctions Cook Book* we've mixed our usual gooey, slimy, fun projects with healthy nutritional choices and sweet treats. With nutrition being an important part of each child's life, we recommend you save the sweet treats for special occasions.

Children will delight in creating our easy-to-make edible concoctions. It is our desire that these activities will provide lifelong memories of the time spent together with a child in your life. As we write this book, our older children are headed off for their college careers away from home. We are so grateful for all of the cherished memories we have created with them throughout our years of concocting.

We would also personally like to thank you for you continued support and affirmation of our Kid Concoctions ventures. We hope this book, as well as all the books in our series, will serve you and your family. Each of us has the ability to enhance a child's life and provide a safe, nurturing, environment in which they can thrive. It is our wish that this book encourages an inspiring relationship with a child in your life.

Happy Concocting!

CONTENTS

**ALL PROJECTS REQUIRE CLOSE
ADULT SUPERVISION OR ASSISTANCE.**

SHAKE & MAKE ICE CREAM

You and your friends or party guests can make delicious ice cream in just minutes.

WHAT YOU WILL NEED:

2 Tbs. sugar
1 cup half-and-half
½ tsp. vanilla extract
6 Tbs. Rock Salt
1 Pint-size plastic zip lock bag
1 Gallon-size plastic zip lock bag
Crushed Ice

HOW TO CONCOCT IT:

1. Combine the sugar, half-and-half and vanilla in the pint-size zip lock bag and seal.

2. Fill the gallon-size zip lock bag one-half full with crushed ice. Add the rock salt.

3. Place the sealed, pint-size zip lock bag into the gallon-size zip lack bag and seal.

4. Shake the gallon-size zip lock bag for 5-7 minutes or until the ice cream hardens.

5. Remove the pint-size bag from the gallon-size bag.

6. Open the pint-size bag and enjoy your ice cream.

CONCOCTION TIPS & IDEAS:

• Make chocolate ice cream by adding 2 Tbs. of chocolate syrup to the ice cream mixture before shaking.

• Try topping your ice cream with sprinkles, nuts, or fresh fruit.

• For a healthier choice use 2% milk in place of half-and-half.

EDIBLE OCEAN

This tasty treat is great for birthday parties and is sure to amaze kids of all ages.

WHAT YOU WILL NEED:

4 cups pre-made blueberry flavored gelatin
4 clear plastic cups
Gummy fish

HOW TO CONCOCT IT:

1. Fill each cup with blueberry flavored gelatin.

2. Gently place 1-2 gummy fish into each cup.

CONCOCTION TIPS & IDEAS:

• Fill a clear plastic party bag with blueberry flavored gelatin, place an orange gummy fish in the center of the gelatin and tie the bag shut with a ribbon. This project looks just like the goldfish in a bag many of us have bought at the carnival or fair.

• Make a large Edible Ocean by filling a new fish bowl full of blueberry gelatin and gummy fish. You can even use grapes for gravel and shoe string licorice for seaweed.

GELATIN ORANGES

These tasty treats look just like real orange wedges and make the perfect low fat snack.

WHAT YOU WILL NEED:

Oranges
1 box of orange flavored gelatin

HOW TO CONCOCT IT:

1. Have an adult cut the oranges in half and scoop out the center leaving the outer skin.

2. Prepare the box of orange gelatin by following the printed instructions on the package.

3. Instead of pouring the liquid gelatin into a bowl to gel, pour it into the orange halves.

4. Place the orange halves full of gelatin into the refrigerator to gel for eight hours.

5. Remove the orange halves from the refrigerator and have an adult cut the oranges into wedges.

CONCOCTION TIPS & IDEAS:

• Use different types of citrus fruits (grapefruit, lemons, and limes) along with different flavors of gelatin to create uniquely tasty treats.

• Follow the directions on the package of gelatin, except try substituting orange juice in place of the water, to create gelatin oranges bursting with flavor.

DOG AND CAT TREATS

Now you can easily create cool and tasty treats that your favorite pet will love.

WHAT YOU WILL NEED:

2 cups whole wheat flour

¼ cup corn meal

½ cup Parmesan cheese

1 medium egg

1 cup water

HOW TO CONCOCT IT:

1. Mix all of the ingredients together, except the ¼ cup of Parmesan cheese. Knead the dough until it is thoroughly mixed.

2. Roll the dough mixture into 3-inch, pencil sized sticks.

3. Roll the dog and cat treats into the remaining Parmesan cheese.

4. If you are making stick-shaped treats, twist the sticks 3-4 times. Then place the treats on an ungreased baking sheet.

5. Bake at 350 degrees for 25-30 minutes.

6. Store dog and cat treats in an airtight container. One batch yields 18-20 small treats.

CONCOCTION TIPS & IDEAS:

• Use a cookie cutter to create Dog and Cat Treats in the shape of animals or dog bones.

• Knead in 8-10 drops of food coloring to add variety to your treats.

GIANT CHOCOLATE SMOOCH

Make a Giant Chocolate Smooch, just like the ones you buy in the store,
that's bound to put a smile on anyone's face.

WHAT YOU WILL NEED:

1 bag of milk chocolate chips
Round funnel
Coffee mug
Non-stick spray
Foil

HOW TO CONCOCT IT:

1. Melt the chocolate chips in the microwave or in a double boiler.

2. Place some tin foil over the small end of the funnel.

3. Place the funnel upright in a coffee mug. Spray the funnel
   with non-stick cooking spray.

4. Pour the melted chocolate into the funnel and place it in the
   freezer for 45 minutes or until the chocolate has hardened completely.

5. Remove the chocolate from the funnel and wrap it in tin foil.

6. Write a message on a narrow piece of paper. Tuck the end of it into the tin foil
   at the point of the Giant Chocolate Smooch.

CONCOCTION TIPS & IDEAS:

• This project requires the assistance and supervision of an adult.

• This project can also be made using white chocolate or peanut butter chips.

• Try wrapping red plastic wrap over the tin foil for an even more festive look.

SODA POP POTION

Our fizzing soda pop concoction will tickle your taste buds and astonish your friends.

WHAT YOU WILL NEED:

4 Tbs. lemon juice

2 tsp. baking soda

2 Tbs. confectioners' sugar

2 quarts cold water

4-6 drops food coloring

HOW TO CONCOCT IT:

1. Stir water, food coloring, confectioners' sugar, and baking soda together in a pitcher until blended.

2. Stir in the lemon juice and your concoction should begin to fizz.

CONCOCTION TIPS & IDEAS:

• Create multicolored ice cubes for your Soda Pop Potion by adding a few drops of food coloring to some water before freezing it in an ice cube tray.

• Make some color change magic by adding blue ice cubes to a yellow Soda Pop Potion. As the ice cubes melt, the soda will turn green!

MONSTER HAND PUNCH

This tasty punch will give your party guests a monster laugh.

WHAT YOU WILL NEED:

6 cups water

1 quart unsweetened grape juice

1 (6 ounce) can of frozen lemonade concentrate

1 (6 ounce) can of frozen orange juice concentrate

2 clean plastic gloves

Green food coloring

HOW TO CONCOCT IT:

1. Mix water, grape juice, lemonade and orange juice together in a large bowl. Place the bowl of fruit punch in the refrigerator.

2. Wash out plastic gloves and fill with water.

3. Add 3-4 drops of food coloring to the water inside the glove.

4. Tie a knot in the top of the glove to keep the water from leaking out. Place the glove in the freezer for 3 hours or until frozen solid.

5. Untie the knot in the gloves and peel the glove away from your monster hands. Place your monster hands into the bowl of fruit punch and serve.

CONCOCTION TIPS & IDEAS:

• Fill a plastic glove with candy, plastic spiders, or other party favors and then tie the end with orange ribbon to create a creepy treat for party guests.

MOVIE GLASS CANDY

Just like the breakable glass used in the movies, only you can eat it, too!

WHAT YOU WILL NEED:

2 cups sugar

1 cup water

Shallow disposable aluminum pan

HOW TO CONCOCT IT:

1. Mix sugar and water together in a small saucepan

2. With the help of an adult, stir the mixture over medium heat until the sugar is dissolved and the mixture is completely clear.

3. Remove the saucepan from the stove and let the liquid cool.

4. Pour the mixture into a shallow disposable aluminum pan.

5. Within 7-10 days the liquid will turn into a sheet of sugar glass.

6. Drain the remaining liquid from the pan. Carefully remove the sugar glass from the pan and place it on several layers of paper towels.

7. Break the Movie Glass with a small hammer, and enjoy a tasty treat.

CONCOCTION TIPS & IDEAS:

• Make Stained Glass Candy by stirring a few drops of food coloring into the candy mixture.

• Remember out Movie Glass is really candy. Real glass is dangerous and should never be eaten under any circumstances!

PEPPERMINT WREATHS

Peppermint wreaths are a great alternative to hanging candy canes on the Christmas tree. These fun treats also make awesome package ties.

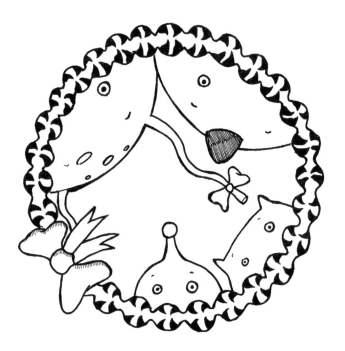

WHAT YOU WILL NEED:

Bag of peppermint discs
Small aluminum pie tins
Cookie sheet
Ribbon

HOW TO CONCOCT IT:

1. Arrange the peppermint discs in pie tins, in the shape of a circle, making sure the discs are touching one another. Place them on the cookie sheet.

2. Place the cookie sheet in a pre-heated oven at 250 degrees for 3-5 minutes or until the peppermint discs melt together.

3. Remove the cookie sheet from the oven and let the Peppermint Wreaths cool for 15 minutes.

4. Use a spatula to carefully remove the cooled Peppermint Wreaths from the pie tins.

5. Use ribbon to tie a bow around the top of the Peppermint Wreaths.

CONCOCTION TIPS & IDEAS:

• Use different types of hard candy and your imagination to create wreaths and other original designs.

GOOEY GUM DROPS

These tasty treats are sure to please even the most selective sweet tooth.

WHAT YOU WILL NEED:

4 Tbs. unflavored gelatin mix

1 cup cold water

1 cup heated fruit juice

3-4 drops peppermint extract

Food coloring

2 cups sugar

HOW TO CONCOCT IT:

1. Mix gelatin, water, extract, and food coloring together in a small bowl. Let the mixture stand for 5 minutes.

2. Add the heated fruit juice to the gelatin mixture. Stir until the gelatin is dissolved.

3. Pour the mixture into a small shallow baking pan.

4. Place the pan into the refrigerator overnight.

5. Cut the Gooey Gum Drops into small squares and then roll in sugar.

CONCOCTION TIPS & IDEAS:

• Experiment by using different flavors of extract to make your Gooey Gum Drops.

• Match the flavor of extract used with the color of food coloring (yellow for lemon, red for peppermint, etc.).

• Ask an adult to help you heat the fruit juice.

FRUITY LEATHER ROLL-UPS

Everyone will enjoy making our updated version of this delicious, classic treat.

WHAT YOU WILL NEED:

2 cups applesauce
¼ cup honey
Non-stick aluminum foil
Cookie sheet
Plastic wrap

HOW TO CONCOCT IT:

1. Stir applesauce and honey together in a small bowl.

2. Line the cookie sheet with the foil.

3. Pour a 1/8" layer of applesauce honey mixture on top of the aluminum foil.

4. Dry the mixture in the oven at 300 degrees for 20 minutes. Let the mixture cool for 3 minutes and then repeat the process until the fruity leather begins to dry. Results may vary depending on the oven you use. Convection settings on the oven work best.

5. After cooling, remove the fruity leather from the cookie sheet. Cut the leather into strips and roll it up, while placing plastic wrap over the fruity leather before rolling it so it will not stick to itself.

CONCOCTION TIPS & IDEAS:

• For added flavor, sprinkle the applesauce honey mixture with a little cinnamon and sugar before placing it in the oven.

CRAZY PRETZELS

Create soft, tasty pretzels in different crazy shapes and sizes.

WHAT YOU WILL NEED:

1 package yeast
1 Tbs. sugar
1 ½ cups warm water
4 cups flour
1 tsp. salt
1 egg, beaten

HOW TO CONCOCT IT:

1. Mix water and yeast together in a large bowl until the yeast dissolves.

2. Add salt, sugar, and flour.

3. Mix and knead the dough until it is smooth.

4. Roll and twist the dough into letters, numbers, and animal shapes.

5. Lay the pretzels on a greased cookie sheet, brush with a beaten egg, then lightly sprinkle with extra salt.

6. Bake at 425 degrees for 12 to 15 minutes.

CONCOCTION TIPS & IDEAS:

• Add a few drops of food coloring to the Crazy Pretzel dough to create rainbow colored pretzels.

PEANUTTY PLAY DOUGH

This is great dough for sculpting edible works of art.

WHAT YOU WILL NEED:

¼ cup peanut butter
½ cup non-fat dry milk
½ Tbs. honey
Plastic zip bag

HOW TO CONCOCT IT:

1. Pour peanut butter, dry milk, and honey into a plastic zip bag.

2. Close bag and knead until the mixture turns to dough.

3. Do not reuse or store Peanutty Play Dough.

CONCOCTION TIPS & IDEAS:

• Use Peanutty Play Dough to create a wide variety of edible sculptures including animals, flowers, and even dinosaurs.

• Use raisins and assorted candies to add eyes, mouths, and other features to your edible creations.

FUNNY FACE TOAST

With this concoction, you can create funny faces, pictures and designs that will brighten up your morning toast.

WHAT YOU WILL NEED:

2 Tbs. milk

2 drops food coloring

Paintbrush

Slice of bread

HOW TO CONCOCT IT:

1. Mix milk and food coloring together in a small dish.

2. Use a paintbrush to paint a face or design on the slice of bread.

3. Toast the bread in a toaster set on the light setting.

CONCOCTION TIPS & IDEAS:

• Funny Face Toast is great when used to make peanut butter and jelly or BLT sandwiches.

• Use Funny Face Toast to kick off a holiday breakfast. Paint a heart on your toast for Valentine's Day, a shamrock for St. Patrick's Day, a pumpkin for Halloween, etc.

PICKLE POTION

With this clever concoction you can transform cucumbers into pickles in just a few hours.

WHAT YOU WILL NEED:

1 large unwashed cucumber
1 Tbs. sugar
2 Tbs. salt
1 cup cider vinegar
Fork

HOW TO CONCOCT IT:

1. Use the prongs of a fork to make deep, lengthwise grooves in the skin of the cucumber.

2. Have an adult slice the cucumber as thin as possible. Paper-thin slices work best.

3. Pour salt into a bowl. Toss the cucumber slices around in the bowl until they are completely covered with salt.

4. Place an airtight cover on top of the bowl. Let the mixture sit for one hour at room temperature.

5. Drain any liquid from the bowl.

6. Mix the sugar and vinegar together and pour it over the cucumbers.

7. Chill the cucumbers in the refrigerator for 3-4 hours and then serve.

CONCOCTION TIPS & IDEAS:

• Try garnishing the pickles with dill before serving.

• Enjoy the pickles on your favorite sandwich or by themselves as a snack.

SWAMP AND SNAKE DESSERT

This *yummy* treat is sure to be a creepy, crawly dessert that kids will love.

WHAT YOU WILL NEED:

1 cup pre-made vanilla pudding

3-4 drops green food coloring

Gummy snakes or worms

2 crushed vanilla wafers

HOW TO CONCOCT IT:

1. Mix pudding and food coloring together in a small bowl until well blended.

2. Spoon the pudding into a small dessert dish.

3. Sprinkle the top of the pudding with the crushed vanilla wafers.

4. Add gummy snakes or worms and serve.

CONCOCTION TIPS & IDEAS:

• Use different colors of food coloring to create Swamp and Snake Desserts in a variety of creepy colors.

• Spice up your Swamp and Snake Dessert by sprinkling mini-marshmallows on top of the pudding.

MAKE YOUR OWN CORN CHIPS

Children will be amazed they can make these delicious corn chips at home.

WHAT YOU WILL NEED:

½ cup yellow cornmeal

½ tsp. salt

1 cup of very hot water

¾ cup of very hot water

1 tsp. margarine

Cookie sheet

HOW TO CONCOCT IT:

1. Mix cornmeal and salt together in a large bowl.

2. Pour in one cup of hot water and margarine, stir until margarine is melted.

3. Add ¾ cup of hot water and stir.

4. Drop spoonfuls of the corn chip mixture onto a greased cookie sheet.

5. Bake at 450 degrees Fahrenheit for 12-15 minutes or until golden brown. Make sure an adult helps you with the oven.

CONCOCTION TIPS & IDEAS:

• Add a few drops of food coloring to your Corn Chips to make a colorful and tasty bowl of chips.

QUICK & EASY SALSA

This classic homemade salsa tastes great and is very easy to make.

WHAT YOU WILL NEED:

2-3 medium tomatoes, chopped

½ cup chopped onions

4-6 chilies serranos
(jalapenos can be substituted)

1/3 cup chopped cilantro

1 tsp. salt

Juice from one-quarter of a fresh lime

HOW TO CONCOCT IT:

1. Mix all of the ingredients together in a small bowl.

2. Cover the mixture and let it sit for one hour before serving.

CONCOCTION TIPS & IDEAS:

• Serve Quick & Easy Salsa with Make Your Own Corn Chips for a tasty snack.

FRUIT KABOBS

You'll love these tasty, nutritious and easy-to-make kabobs.

WHAT YOU WILL NEED:

Bamboo skewers

Grapes (washed and removed from the stem)

Bananas (peeled and sliced)

Can of pineapple chunks (drained)

Can of mandarin oranges (drained)

HOW TO CONCOCT IT:

1. Sort each type of fruit into a different bowl.

2. Create unique and colorful patterns by pushing pieces of fruit onto the skewers.

3. Serve Fruit Kabobs by themselves or with plain yogurt for dipping.

CONCOCTION TIPS & IDEAS:

• Create an interesting centerpiece for the dinner table by pushing Fruit Kabobs into a large honeydew melon or cantaloupe.

• Experiment by making Fruit Kabobs with different types of fruit like strawberries, blueberries, watermelons, etc.

BIRD COOKIES

Our feathered friends chirp over these tasty cookie treats that are for the birds.

WHAT YOU WILL NEED:

1 hard bagel
Creamy peanut butter
Mixed birdseed
Twine

HOW TO CONCOCT IT:

1. Cover the bagel with peanut butter.

2. Roll the bagel over the birdseed so that it is completely covered.

3. Tie the twine around the bagel, and hang it on a tree limb.

CONCOCTION TIPS & IDEAS:

• Make another great bird treat by covering a pine cone with peanut butter instead.

MINTY GREEN SHAKE

Children of all ages will enjoy this minty ice cold shake.

WHAT YOU WILL NEED:

1 cup milk

1 scoop vanilla ice cream

2 ice cubes

3-4 drops mint extract to taste

2 drops green food coloring

HOW TO CONCOCT IT:

1. Place milk, ice cream, and ice cubes in a blender and blend on high for 10 seconds.

2. Add mint extract and 2 drops of green food coloring and blend for an additional 10 seconds.

3. Pour your Minty Green Shake into a glass and serve.

CONCOCTION TIPS & IDEAS:

• Spice up your shake by adding a little whipped cream and a cherry on top.

• Change the flavors of your shake by substituting vanilla extract, chocolate syrup, etc. in place of the mint extract.

• Give your shake a little zing by adding a splash of seltzer water.

DIVING RAISINS SODA

Turn a dull glass of soda pop into a mini-tank of scuba diving raisins.

WHAT YOU WILL NEED:

1 glass clear soda pop (ginger ale, club soda, etc.)
Raisins

HOW TO CONCOCT IT:

1. Add several raisins to the glass of clear soda pop

2. Watch as the raisins dive and resurface just like little scuba divers.

CONCOCTION TIPS & IDEAS:

• Add 1 tsp. of baking soda to your glass of soda and the raisins will dive and resurface even faster.

PUDDIN' PAINT

Budding young artists will enjoy this wonderful "first paint."

WHAT YOU WILL NEED:

1 large packet of instant vanilla pudding
2 cups ice cold water
Food coloring

HOW TO CONCOCT IT:

1. Whisk water and instant pudding together in a bowl for 2 minutes.

2. Refrigerate for 5 minutes.

3. Divide the pudding into several small bowls or muffin tins.

4. Add 5-7 drops of food coloring to each bowl or tin and mix.

CONCOCTION TIPS & IDEAS:

• Use Puddin' Paints along with other paints in this book to create really cool works of art.

• Puddin' Paints also double as a fantastic finger paint!

POTATO DOUGH

We came up with this dough while figuring out what to do with leftover mashed potatoes. Although we don't recommend eating this recipe, it is a lot of fun to play with.

WHAT YOU WILL NEED:

2 cups mashed potatoes

1 ½ cups flour

4-6 drops of food coloring

HOW TO CONCOCT IT:

1. Mix mashed potatoes and flour together in a large bowl.

2. Add 4-6 drops of food coloring and stir until the color is evenly blended.

3. Use Potato Dough as you would any other type of dough, but do not store or reuse Potato Dough.

CONCOCTION TIPS & IDEAS:

• Add a few drops of extract or 1 Tbs. of unsweetened drink mix to give Potato Dough a wide variety of different scents and colors. If using drink mix, omit the food coloring from the concoction.

CANDY JEWELRY

Create bright colored necklaces and bracelets you can wear and eat.

WHAT YOU WILL NEED:

Shoe string licorice

Cereal with holes in the middle

Hard candy with holes in the middle

HOW TO CONCOCT IT:

1. Cut a piece of shoe string licorice to the desired length. Make sure the licorice is longer for a necklace or shorter for a bracelet.

2. String cereal and hard candy onto the shoe string licorices, creating different designs and patterns.

3. Tie the loose ends of the licorice together around your neck or wrist.

CONCOCTION TIPS & IDEAS:

• Candy Jewelry make great birthday favors or a wonderful activity for a slumber party.

• You can also string marshmallows onto the licorice for more variation. Use a bobby pin to poke a hole in the middle of the marshmallow and then string it onto the licorice.

KOOKIE COOKIE PAINT

With this wacky and wild concoction, young Picassos can actually eat their works of art.

WHAT YOU WILL NEED:

1 beaten egg yolk
4-6 drops of food coloring
Store bought sugar cookie dough
Wax paper
Paintbrushes

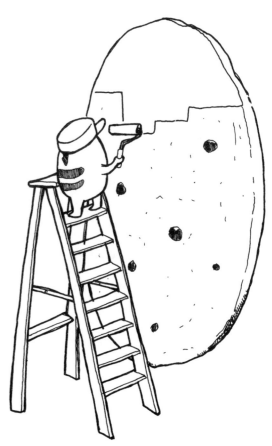

HOW TO CONCOCT IT:

1. Mix the egg yolk and food coloring together in a small bowl. Repeat this process several times to create different colors of Kookie Cookie Paint.

2. Roll the cookie dough out on wax paper and cut with assorted shapes and sizes of cookie cutters.

3. Place the cookies on a greased cookie sheet.

4. Using your Kookie Cookie Paints and paintbrushes, you can create various different designs and pictures on your cookies.

5. Bake as directed on the package of cookie dough.

CONCOCTION TIPS & IDEAS:

• Before baking, sprinkle cookies with colored sugar or candy sprinkles.

COOKIE BOUQUET

Instead of giving someone a bouquet of flowers,
why not try giving them this fun-to-make Cookie Bouquet?

WHAT YOU WILL NEED:

1 package (18 ounces) refrigerated chocolate chip cookie dough

8 flat wooden sticks

HOW TO CONCOCT IT:

1. Pre-heat oven to 375 degrees Fahrenheit.

2. Roll the dough into eight, 2-inch balls. Place the balls on an ungreased cookie sheet.

3. Insert the wooden sticks into each ball so they look like a lollipop.

4. Bake 13 to 15 minutes or until the edges of the cookies are crisp.

5. Ask an adult to help you take the cookies out of the oven and then help them transfer the cookies to a wire rack. Allow them to cool completely.

6. Put your cookies together to form a bouquet and give them as a gift.

CONCOCTION TIPS & IDEAS:

• Jazz up your cookie bouquet by tying a ribbon around each stick, and then wrap each cookie in colored plastic wrap.

• Arrange you Cookie Bouquet in a small glass vase or floral box just as you would a real bouquet of flowers.

STAINED GLASS COOKIES

These tasty cookies look like stained glass and taste like candy!

WHAT YOU WILL NEED:

1 package of pre-made sugar cookie dough
Hard candy (Lifesavers® or Jolly Ranchers®)
Zip lock bags
Rolling pin
2 cookie cutters

HOW TO CONCOCT IT:

1. Roll out the cookie dough and cut out cookies using the larger cookie cutter. Then, use the smaller cookie cutter to cut a hole in the center of each cookie.

2. Place the cookies on a foil covered cookie sheet.

3. Put the hard candies into the plastic zip lock bag and crush them using the rolling pin.

4. Use the crushed candy to fill the holes in the center of the cookies.

5. Get an adult to help you bake your cookies at 375 degrees Fahrenheit for 8-10 minutes until lightly brown. Cool completely and then peel the cookies off the foil.

CONCOCTION TIPS & IDEAS:

• Make this project using holiday shaped cookie cutters and colored candies, such as heart-shaped cookie cutters and red candy for Valentine's Day or shamrock cookie cutters and green candy for St. Patrick's Day.

SHAKE AND MAKE BUTTER

Have a blast creating tasty butter in minutes by shaking a zip bag full of kitchen ingredients.

WHAT YOU WILL NEED:

1 large zip bag or plastic container with lid
1 pint heavy whipping cream
1 pinch of salt

HOW TO CONCOCT IT:

1. Pour the heavy whipping cream and salt into the large zip bag or container.

2. Seal the bag or container.

3. After 15 minutes of shaking the zip bag or container, chunks of butter will begin to form.

4. Drain the excess liquid from the zip bag or container, and then seal it.

5. Store the butter in the refrigerator until you are ready to use it.

CONCOCTION TIPS & IDEAS:

• Push Shake & Make butter chunks into a candy mold, place it in the refrigerator, and pop your shaped butter out when it is hard.

• Add 1 Tbs. of honey or maple syrup to add more flavor to your Shake & Make Butter.

SWEETHEART CHOCOLATE ROSES

These Sweetheart Chocolate Roses are not only beautiful to look at, they're also good to eat!

WHAT YOU WILL NEED:

Bag of small chocolate kisses
Red or pink plastic wrap
Clear tape
Green pipe cleaners
Green tissue paper

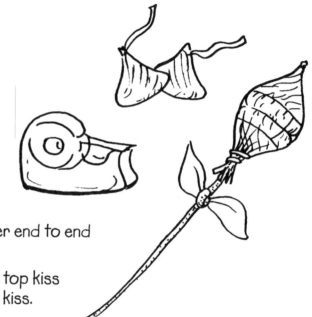

HOW TO CONCOCT IT:

1. First make your rose bud by taping two, foil wrapped kisses together end to end with plastic tape.

2. Cut and wrap a 5-inch square of plastic wrap over the point of the top kiss and gather the edges twisting into a tail at the point of the bottom kiss.

3. Twist the top of a green pipe cleaner around the tail to form a stem.

4. Add leaves by twisting the pipe cleaner once around the center of a green strip of tissue paper.

5. Cut each end of the tissue paper strip so that the tissue paper resembles rose leaves.
   Repeat the above steps several times to make a bouquet of Sweetheart Chocolate Roses.

CONCOCTION TIPS & IDEAS:

• Arrange several Sweetheart Chocolate Roses in a vase with real greens to give it as a fancy gift.

• Use different colors of plastic wrap to create a bouquet of roses in assorted colors.

• You can also use old, inexpensive plastic roses for the stems, by removing the flower from the top and taping your chocolate kisses on the recycled stem.

TASTY TAFFY

This concoction captures the taste of old-fashioned taffy.

WHAT YOU WILL NEED:

1 cup sugar

¼ cup water

2 Tbs. vinegar

1 Tbs. butter

½ tsp. vanilla extract

HOW TO CONCOCT IT:

1. Mix the sugar, water, and vinegar together in a large pot.

2. Have an adult boil the mixture until it reaches the "hard ball stage" (a drop of the mixture turns into a ball when dropped in cold water).

3. Stir in the butter and vanilla and then pour the mixture into a shallow pan coated with butter.

4. Let the mixture cool for one hour.

5. Butter your hands and then twist, pull, and fold the mixture until it becomes a creamy color and is difficult to pull.

6. Roll the taffy into a long rope and then cut into small pieces and wrap in wax paper.

CONCOCTION TIPS & IDEAS:

• Try adding a few drops of food coloring to the sugar, water and vinegar mixture to make your taffy different colors.

• Put a handful of homemade Tasty Taffy into a glass jar and give it as a gift.

CANDY CLAY

Not only can you sculpt with this awesome clay, you can eat it too!

WHAT YOU WILL NEED:

1 pound powered sugar
1/3 cup corn syrup
½ tsp. salt
1/3 cup margarine (softened)
1 tsp. vanilla extract
5-7 drops of food coloring

HOW TO CONCOCT IT:

1. Mix all ingredients together in a small bowl until blended. If the mixture is too sticky, add more powdered sugar.

2. Sculpt with your Candy Clay to create different animals, pretend fruits, and other sculptures you can eat!

CONCOCTION TIPS & IDEAS:

• Experiment by using different colors and different flavors of extract (banana, almond, etc.).

• Use Candy Clay sculptures to decorate the top of your favorite dessert.

CHOCOLATE CLAY

With this concoction, you can sculpt and eat your incredible clay creations.

WHAT YOU WILL NEED:

10 oz. semi-sweet chocolate chips
1/3 cup light corn syrup

HOW TO CONCOCT IT:

1. Pour chocolate chips into a microwave safe bowl and place in the microwave on High for 1 minute.

2. Stir the chocolate and place back in the microwave for 1 minute or until the chocolate is melted.

3. Stir in the corn syrup.

4. Spread the chocolate out ½ inch thick on a sheet of wax of paper.

5. Let the chocolate set overnight. It will stiffen and become pliable. Now you are ready to sculpt!

CONCOCTION TIPS & IDEAS:

• Make Chocolate Clay in a wide variety of different colors by using white chocolate chips and stirring in a few drops of food coloring before the corn syrup is added.

FROSTING DOUGH

This edible dough is a fantastic way to top off any birthday cake or cupcake.

WHAT YOU WILL NEED:

1 can frosting
1 ½ cups powdered sugar
1 cup peanut butter
6-8 drops food coloring

HOW TO CONCOCT IT:

1. Mix frosting, powdered sugar, food coloring and peanut butter together in a large bowl.

2. Knead the mixture until it turns into a dough.

3. Mold with Frosting Dough as you would any other dough.

CONCOCTION TIPS & IDEAS:

• Use Frosting Dough to create animals, people, flowers, and other unique works of edible art.

• Frosting Dough sculptures can be used to garnish desserts such as cake, pies, and ice cream.

WHIPPED CREAM FINGER PAINT

This delicious finger paint is a fun way to introduce small children to finger painting.

WHAT YOU WILL NEED:

¼ cup whipped cream
2-4 drops food coloring
Freezer paper

HOW TO CONCOCT IT:

1. Mix whipped cream and food coloring together in a small bowl. Repeat this step to create various colors of Whipped Cream Finger Paint.

2. Finger paint on the shiny side of the freezer paper; it works just as well as store bought finger painting paper and it's a lot loss expensive.

CONCOCTION TIPS & IDEAS:

• Add a drop of vanilla, peppermint, or banana extract to give Whipped Cream Finger Paint a wonderful scent and a great taste.

• The whipped topping in the plastic tubs works great for this recipe.

GUMDROP ORNAMENTS

These pretty gumdrop ornaments not only look great, they taste pretty good too.

WHAT YOU WILL NEED:

Small round foam ball
Toothpicks
Gumdrops
String

HOW TO CONCOCT IT:

1. Push 3 gumdrops onto a toothpick, leaving one end of the toothpick exposed.

2. Push the exposed end of the toothpick into the foam ball. Repeat the above steps several times, until you have made enough gumdrop toothpicks to cover the entire ball.

3. Tie a string around the Gumdrop Ornament and hang it up for decoration.

CONCOCTION TIPS & IDEAS:

• Make unique ornaments by arranging different color gumdrops in various patterns on the foam ball.

• Use a cone shaped piece of foam to create a gumdrop tree.

CHOCOLATE FUDGE COCOA

This has been a favorite drink in our family for years.
Made with three kinds of chocolate, it's a chocolate lover's dream come true.

WHAT YOU WILL NEED:

½ gallon white milk
2/3 cup milk chocolate chips
6 Tbs. cocoa powder
1/3 cup sugar
1 quart chocolate milk

HOW TO CONCOCT IT:

1. Mix 1 cup of the white milk, the chocolate chips, the cocoa, and the sugar together in a large saucepan. Cook over low heat until the sugar dissolves.

2. Add the rest of the white milk and all of the chocolate milk. Stir the mixture until it begins to steam. Do not let the cocoa boil!

3. Pour into cups and serve. If the cocoa is too hot, let it cool before drinking. Makes 12 servings.

CONCOCTION TIPS & IDEAS:

• This project requires help and supervision from an adult.

• Top your Chocolate Fudge Cocoa with miniature marshmallows or fresh whipped cream.

• A thermos full of Chocolate Fudge Cocoa with a gift tag attached containing the recipe makes an awesome gift!

BIRTHDAY CAKE COOKIES

These wonderful cookies are easy to make and taste just like a birthday cake..

WHAT YOU WILL NEED:

1 box cake mix

2 eggs

½ cup vegetable oil

Nuts & chocolate chips (optional)

HOW TO CONCOCT IT:

1. Mix oil, eggs and cake mix together in a large bowl.

2. Stir in chocolate chips and nuts

3. Drop tablespoon size mounds of batter onto a greased cookie sheet.

4. Get an adult to help you bake in a pre-heated oven at 350 degrees Fahrenheit for 10 minutes.

CONCOCTION TIPS & IDEAS:

• Experiment by using different flavors of cake mix.

• Decorate your Birthday Cake Cookies with frosting and candy sprinkles.

EDIBLE GREETING CARD

Why give a regular paper card when you can give this easy-to-make Edible Card?

WHAT YOU WILL NEED:

1 package pre-made sugar cookie dough
1 beaten egg yolk
Cookie sheet
Food coloring
Small paint brushes

HOW TO CONCOCT IT:

1. Mix the egg yolk and food coloring together in a small bowl. Repeat this process several times to make different colors of paint.

2. Roll the cookie dough out on a greased cookie sheet.

3. Cut and shape the dough to the size card desired.

4. Use the small paint brushes and the egg yolk/food coloring mixture to write a message and paint a design on the card.

5. Ask an adult to help you bake as directed on the package of cookie dough.

CONCOCTION TIPS & IDEAS:

• Add pizzazz to your Edible Card by sprinkling it with candy sprinkle or colored sugar before baking.

• Wrap your Edible Card with colorful plastic wrap and tie a ribbon around it.

CHOCOLATE PRETZEL STICKS

These tasty chocolate covered pretzels make the perfect sweet and salty snack.

WHAT YOU WILL NEED:

1 cup milk chocolate chips
Pretzel rods
Candy sprinkles
Microwave safe bowl
Wax paper

HOW TO CONCOCT IT:

1. Pour chocolate chips into the microwave safe
   bowl and place it in the microwave for 3 minutes
   or until the chocolate has melted. Have an adult remove
   the bowl from the microwave and stir.

2. Use a spoon to drizzle the chocolate over half of the pretzel
   rod and then sprinkle with the candy sprinkles.

3. Set the pretzel rods on wax paper for 30 minutes or until the chocolate has hardened.

CONCOCTION TIPS & IDEAS:

• Use different types and colors of candy or crushed nuts to Chocolate Pretzel Sticks
   for holidays and special occasions.

• Try making pretzels sticks using white chocolate chips or peanut butter chips.

CHOCOLATE SPOONS

Chocolate Spoons are great for eating ice cream or stirring hot cocoa.

WHAT YOU WILL NEED:

1 cup milk chocolate chips

12 plastic spoons

Wax paper

HOW TO CONCOCT IT:

1. Pour the chocolate chips in a microwavable bowl and place in the microwave for 5 minutes on the Medium setting. Remove from the microwave and stir.

2. Keep repeating the above process until the chocolate chips are melted.

3. Dip the end of the plastic spoons into the melted chocolate and place them on a sheet of wax paper to harden.

CONCOCTION TIPS & IDEAS:

• Try rolling your Chocolate Spoons in nuts and sprinkles before they harden.

• Turn your Chocolate Spoons into tasty gifts by wrapping the chocolate covered end of the spoon in plastic wrap and tying it with a ribbon.

MELT AWAY MARSHMALLOWS

These marshmallows are so delicious, you will never eat store bought marshmallows again.

WHAT YOU WILL NEED:

½ cup powder confectioners' sugar

3 Tbs. cornstarch

2 cups granulated sugar

3 envelopes unflavored gelatin

¼ tsp. salt

1 cup cold water

1 tsp. clear vanilla extract

HOW TO CONCOCT IT:

1. Mix powder sugar and cornstarch together in a small bowl.

2. Butter a 9x9 baking pan. Coat the pan with 1/3 of the cornstarch and powder sugar mixture, making sure the bottom and sides are covered.

3. Mix granulated sugar, gelatin and salt together in a medium saucepan. Stir in cold water and let stand for 5 minutes.

4. Stir over low heat, until the sugar dissolves. Remove from heat.

5. After the mixture has cooled, stir in vanilla extract.

6. Pour the mixture in a large bowl and beat with an electric mixer for 12 minutes or until soft peaks are formed.

7. Pour the mixture into the 9x9 baking pan. Let the mixture sit overnight at room temperature.

8. Cut the marshmallows into squares and roll in the remaining sugar / cornstarch mixture.

CONCOCTION TIPS & IDEAS:

• Add a few drops of food coloring to the mixture in step 6 to create colored marshmallows for various different holidays.

BANANA POPS

Just like the cold tasty treats sold at many fairs and amusement parks.

WHAT YOU WILL NEED:

Bananas

8 oz Chocolate syrup

Chopped walnuts or pecans (optional)

Popsicle sticks

HOW TO CONCOCT IT:

1. Peel bananas and cut in half. Insert a popsicle stick into the bottom of each banana half.

2. Pour the chocolate syrup into a large bowl. Hold the banana pop over the bowl and spoon chocolate syrup over the banana until it is completely covered.

3. Fill a small baking pan with finely chopped nuts. Roll the chocolate covered banana into the mixture.

4. Lay the banana pops on a pan covered with wax paper and freeze for 4-6 hours.

CONCOCTION TIPS & IDEAS:

• For a healthy alternative cover the banana pop with yogurt instead of chocolate syrup.

• Try making pops with other types of fruit including: pineapple, peaches, and strawberries.

QUICK & EASY PIZZA

This delicious project is a wonderful way to introduce children to cooking.

WHAT YOU WILL NEED:

English muffins
1 jar pizza sauce
1 package shredded mozzarella cheese

HOW TO CONCOCT IT:

1. Cut English muffins in half and toast.

2. Place muffins on a cookie sheet covered with tin foil.

3. Spread pizza sauce onto the muffin and sprinkle with cheese.

4. Place in the oven and broil for 2-3 minutes, or until cheese melts.

CONCOCTION TIPS & IDEAS:

• Have a pizza party. Make a topping bar by filling several small bowls with various different pizza toppings including: pepperoni, green peppers, onions, mushrooms and tomatoes. You and your guests will have fun creating your own made to order pizzas.

ASTRONAUT PUDDING

This is a great project that children love to
make for birthday parties, or when learning about space.

WHAT YOU WILL NEED:

1 Tbs. instant pudding
¼ cup of ice cold milk
Pint-size plastic zip lock bag

HOW TO CONCOCT IT:

1. Pour milk and 1 Tbs. of instant pudding into the plastic zip bag.

2. Seal the zip bag. Squeeze out as much air as possible before
   closing the bag.

3. Knead the bag for 3-5 minutes until the milk and instant pudding
   are well blended.

4. Snip the corner of the zip bag with a pair of scissors and
   squeeze the pudding into your mouth

CONCOCTION TIPS & IDEAS:

• Have more astronaut fun by eating other foods like Jell-O®
  or ice cream out of a zip bag.

SPAGHETTI ICE CREAM

This tasty ice cream treat looks like a real sauce covered pile of spaghetti.

WHAT YOU WILL NEED:

Vanilla ice cream (slightly softened)

Cookie press with die containing several medium size holes

Strawberry topping

HOW TO CONCOCT IT:

1. Spoon the vanilla ice cream into the cookie press.

2. Squeeze out the ice cream into long strands on to a plate so it resembles spaghetti.

3. Quickly top with strawberry topping and serve.

CONCOCTION TIPS & IDEAS:

• Sprinkle a little shredded coconut on top of the strawberry topping to resemble Parmesan cheese.

BANANA HOT DOGS

Banana Hot Dogs have been a favorite in our family for years.
The make great lunch box sandwiches.

WHAT YOU WILL NEED:

Banana
Hot dog bun
Peanut butter

HOW TO CONCOCT IT:

1. Spread a thin layer of peanut butter on the inside of the hot dog bun.

2. Peel the banana.

3. Place the banana inside the hot dog bun. Enjoy!

CONCOCTION TIPS & IDEAS:

• Try topping your banana hot dog with raisins and other types of dried fruit.

PEANUT BUTTER & RAISIN STUFFED APPLES

Peanut Butter & Raisin Stuffed Apples are healthy yummy treats the entire family will enjoy!

WHAT YOU WILL NEED:

Green Granny Smith apple
2 Tbs. peanut butter
1 Tbs. raisins

HOW TO CONCOCT IT:

1. Cut the top inch off of the apple to make a lid.

2. Set the lid aside and core the remaining piece of the apple without making a hole through the bottom of the apple. A grapefruit spoon works great for this step and it is safer than a knife.

3. Mix the peanut butter and raisins together in a small bowl.

4. Spoon the peanut butter and raisin mixture into the apple and top with the apple lid.

CONCOCTION TIPS & IDEAS:

• Try adding other types of dried fruit and chopped nuts to the peanut butter for an even more unique snack.

FOSSIL SUCKERS

These mouthwatering candy treats look like real creatures fossilized in amber.

WHAT YOU WILL NEED:

12 lollipop sticks

Gummy Candy (fish, worms, bugs etc.)

2 cups sugar

¾ cup light corn syrup

¾ cup water

2 tsp. extract

1 drop yellow food coloring

Candy thermometer

HOW TO CONCOCT IT:

1. Push each lollipop stick into 1-2 gummy candies.

2. Arrange the sticks on a cookie sheet.

3. Stir corn syrup, sugar, and water in a pot over medium heat until all of the sugar dissolves.

4. Stop stirring. Boil the mixture until the candy thermometer reads between 300 degrees – 310 degrees. IMMEDIATELY remove from heat!

5. Stir in extract and food coloring.

6. Quickly spoon 1-2 Tbs. of the mixture over the gummy candy and the top of the stick. Let the suckers cool for 2 hours or until completely hard.

CONCOCTION TIPS & IDEAS:

• Experiment by using different colors of food coloring. For example, use green food coloring and gummy worms to create "Slimy Worm Suckers".

SLOPPY JOE BISCUIT POTS

This recipe is a family favorite for 4th of July picnics and birthday parties.

WHAT YOU WILL NEED:

2 lbs. pre-made Sloppy Joe mix
1 can of refrigerated biscuits (10 biscuits)
Shredded cheddar cheese

HOW TO CONCOCT IT:

1. Pre-heat over to 400 degrees.

2. Press biscuits into 10 un-greased standard size muffin cups. Press dough firmly on the bottom and up the sides of the cup.

3. Spoon ¼ cup of the Sloppy Joe mixture into each biscuit cup.

4. Bake at 400 degrees for 10 minutes or until the edges of the biscuits are golden brown.

5. Sprinkle cheese on top of each biscuit cup and continue baking until cheese is melted. Let stand 1-2 minutes before removing from the pan

CONCOCTION TIPS & IDEAS:

• Experiment by filling the biscuit pots with other types of ingredients including: diced hot dogs & cheese, lightly cooked scrambled eggs & cheese, pizza sauce with pepperoni & mozzarella cheese etc.

YOGURT & FRUIT CREPE ROLLS

These healthy crepes are sweet enough for desert and nutritional enough for breakfast.

WHAT YOU WILL NEED:

Pre-made crepes
Vanilla flavored yogurt
Sliced strawberries
Blueberries

HOW TO CONCOCT IT:

1. Spread a thin layer of yogurt on each crepe.

2. Evenly layer sliced strawberries and blue berries on top of the yogurt.

3. Roll the crepe up around the fruit and yogurt. Enjoy!

CONCOCTION TIPS & IDEAS:

• Customize your Yogurt & Fruit Crepes by using various different flavors of yogurt and different types of fruit.

YUMMY MAC & CHEESE

A quick and easy version of a classic children's favorite.

WHAT YOU WILL NEED:

1 pound cooked & drained elbow macaroni

3 cups half & half

14 Ritz® crackers

18 slices American cheese or cheddar cheese

1 tsp. salt, pepper and paprika

HOW TO CONCOCT IT:

1. Pre-Heat the oven to 350 degrees.

2. Coat a 9 x 13 inch baking pan with butter.

3. Pour 1/3 of the pasta into the pan and cover with 1 cup half & half and 6 slices of cheese. Repeat this step 2 more times to create 3 different layers.

4. Place the crackers along with the salt, pepper and paprika in a zip bag. Seal the bag and crush up the crackers.

5. Sprinkle the cracker crumbs over the top layer and bake for 30 to 40 minutes. Serves 6.

CONCOCTION TIPS & IDEAS:

• Use 3 different colors of macaroni to create Neapolitan Mac & Cheese.

• Try mixing in chopped broccoli or diced tomatoes with the pasta before creating the different layers.

ICE CREAM CONE CUPCAKES

These delicious cup cakes look like real ice cream cones and are great for birthday parties.

WHAT YOU WILL NEED:

1 box of pre-made cake mix (follow directions on the box)
Regular ice cream cones (flat on the bottom)
White or chocolate frosting

HOW TO CONCOCT IT:

1. Pre-heat the oven to 350 degrees.

2. Fill each ice cream cone half full with cake batter.

3. Place the cones on a baking sheet and carefully place them in the oven.

4. Bake for 25 minutes or until a tooth pick is inserted into the cake and comes out clean.

5. Let the cones cool and then cover the tops with frosting.

CONCOCTION TIPS & IDEAS:

• Decorate the Ice Cream Cone Cupcakes with various types of candy including gummies, sprinkles, and mini chocolate chips.

TREASURE POPCORN BALLS

Popcorn balls with tasty treats hidden inside.

WHAT YOU WILL NEED:

2 cups plain popcorn, popped

½ cup corn syrup

½ cup sugar

Butter

Candy treats; candy rings, candy necklaces, gummies etc.

HOW TO CONCOCT IT:

1. Stir corn syrup and sugar in a pot over medium heat. Continue stirring until all of the sugar is dissolved.

2. Let the mixture cool. Pour the mixture over the bowl of popcorn until evenly coated, but not soggy.

3. Butter your hands and mold the popcorn around various candy treats into the shape of a ball.

4. Wrap the popcorn balls in wax paper.

CONCOCTION TIPS & IDEAS:

• Add a few drops of food coloring to the corn syrup and sugar mixture to create colored Treasure Popcorn Balls.

BEACH IN A CUP

Create a mini beach scene that is fun to look at and even more fun to eat.

WHAT YOU WILL NEED:

1 cup pre-made vanilla pudding

½ cup vanilla wafers

Small drink umbrella

Small gumball (this will be your beach ball)

HOW TO CONCOCT IT:

1. Spoon the vanilla pudding into a clear plastic cup.

2. Sprinkle the crushed vanilla wafers on top of the pudding.

3. Add the drink umbrella and gumball to accessorize your beach scene.

CONCOCTION TIPS & IDEAS:

• Mix in a few drops of blue food coloring with the vanilla pudding before spooning it into the cup. This will create the look of a floating "Desert Island Dessert."

TASTY TACO SOUP

This flavorful soup is easy to make and is great when served with biscuits or corn chips.

WHAT YOU WILL NEED:

1 lb. ground beef
1 can chopped tomatoes
1 can kidney red beans
1 can pinto beans
1 can white corn
1 envelope taco seasoning
1 envelope ranch dressing mix

HOW TO CONCOCT IT:

1. Brown the ground beef in a skillet and drain.

2. Mix the ground beef and the rest of the ingredients together in a large pot and sinner for 30 minutes.

CONCOCTION TIPS & IDEAS:

• Tasty Taco Soup also makes a great party dip when served with tortilla chips.

• Serve your soup topped with shredded cheddar cheese and crushed corn chips.

JUICY POPSICLES

Juicy Popsicles tickle the taste buds with an explosion of flavor and are the perfect treat on a hot summer day.

WHAT YOU WILL NEED:

Apple juice
Grape juice
Popsicle sticks
Wax coated cups
Plastic wrap

HOW TO CONCOCT IT:

1. Fill a wax coated cup half full with grape juice.

2. Cover the cup with a piece of plastic wrap.

3. Poke a popsicle stick through the center of the plastic wrap until it reaches the bottom of the cup. Freeze for 2 hours or until solid.

4. Remove plastic wrap and fill the cup the rest of the way full with apple juice. Freeze until solid.

5. Peel the wax cup off of the popsicle and enjoy.

CONCOCTION TIPS & IDEAS:

• Experiment by mixing various different flavors of fruit juice.

FRUIT SOUP

A refreshing summer snack children and adults of all ages will enjoy!

WHAT YOU WILL NEED:

Honeydew

1 banana

Plums

Kiwi fruit

Grapes

Sliced strawberries

2 cups orange juice

1 scoop frozen sorbet

HOW TO CONCOCT IT:

1. Scoop balls from the honeydew melon using a ball cutter.

2. Wash, peel and cut up the remaining fruit.

3. Pour orange juice and banana into a blender and mix for 60 seconds or until smooth.

4. Divide the mixture into 3-4 small bowls. Add cut up fruit and top with a scoop of sorbet.

CONCOCTION TIPS & IDEAS:

• Create a Tropical Fruit Soup by adding chunks of pineapple and coconut.

FRUITY FUN DIP

This delicious dip is a wonderful compliment to all different types of fresh fruit.

WHAT YOU WILL NEED:

1 32 oz. jar marshmallow cream

1 8 oz container of fruit flavored cream cheese (strawberry)

HOW TO CONCOCT IT:

1. In a medium bowl, mix the marshmallow cream and cream cheese together with an electric mixer until smooth.

2. Refrigerate the mixture for at least one hour.

3. Serve with fresh fruit.

CONCOCTION TIPS & IDEAS:

• Favorite fruits for dipping include; strawberries, grapes, sliced bananas, and peeled / sliced kiwi.

BANANA CHIPS

Banana Chips are a great snack on the go and a healthy alternative to potato chips.

WHAT YOU WILL NEED:

2 sliced ripe bananas
Honey

HOW TO CONCOCT IT:

1. Pre-heat the oven to 150 degrees.

2. Spray a cookie sheet with cooking spray.

3. Arrange the banana slices in a single layer on the cookie sheet.

4. Brush with a thin light layer of honey.

5. Cook for 2 hours with the oven door open 1 inch. Flip each slice with a fork and cook 2 more hours.

6. Bananas are done when they are hard and can no longer bend. Store in a plastic zip bag.

CONCOCTION TIPS & IDEAS:

• Combine banana chips raisins, and nuts together in a zip bag to create a delicious trail mix.

CHICKEN & SHOOTING STARS SOUP

This quick and easy recipe is a fun spin on classic chicken noodle soup

WHAT YOU WILL NEED:

1 medium carrot (washed & cut into ¼ inch slices)

4 cups chicken broth

¼ cup star shaped pasta

¾ cup diced, cooked chicken

Salt & pepper

HOW TO CONCOCT IT:

1. In a medium pot bring the broth to a simmer over medium heat.

2. Add carrots and simmer for 10 minutes.

3. Stir in pasta and chicken. Simmer for 7-10 more minutes or until pasta is tender.

4. Add salt and pepper to taste.

CONCOCTION TIPS & IDEAS:

• Mix in various different sizes and shapes of pasta.

• Cut carrots into the shape of a star.

SHERBET WATERMELON SLICES

This sherbet dessert looks like real slices of watermelon will amaze your friends.

WHAT YOU WILL NEED:

Lime sherbet
Raspberry sherbet
Chocolate chips

HOW TO CONCOCT IT:

1. Line a clear glass bowl with plastic wrap.

2. Smooth ¾-inch layer of lime sherbet around the bottom and the sides of the bowl to form the watermelon rind.

3. Freeze for 1 hour or until hard.

4. Mix softened raspberry sherbet and chocolate chips together in a separate bowl.

5. Spoon the mixture inside of the lime sherbet rind and freeze for 2 hours.

6. Dip the bottom of the bowl into room temperature water to loosen the watermelon.

7. Turn the bowl upside down on a plate to remove the watermelon from the bowl. Slice & serve.

CONCOCTION TIPS & IDEAS:

• Serve with a mix of fresh blueberries, raspberries and blackberries.

PEANUT BUTTER CRUNCH COOKIES

Crunchy cookies that are quick, easy and fun for the entire family to make and eat together.

WHAT YOU WILL NEED:

½ cup sugar

½ cup corn syrup

1 cup peanut butter

3 cups corn flakes

HOW TO CONCOCT IT:

1. Stir sugar and corn syrup together in a saucepan over medium heat until the sugar dissolves.

2. Remove from heat. Add peanut butter and stir until well blended.

3. Add corn flakes and stir until well coated.

4. Drop spoonfuls of the mixture on a cookie sheet covered with wax paper and allow to cool.

CONCOCTION TIPS & IDEAS:

• Add 1/8 cup raisins to step 3 to create Peanut Butter Raisin Crunch Cookies.

PICTURE FRAME TOAST

A tasty breakfast treat that looks like a framed work of art.

WHAT YOU WILL NEED:

1 slice of bread
Softened butter
1 medium egg
Cookie cutter

HOW TO CONCOCT IT:

1. Spread a thin layer of butter on one side on the bread.

2. Firmly press the cookie cutter into the center of the bread, remove the cut image.

3. Lay both pieces of bread on a cookie sheet, buttered side up.

4. Break the egg open into a small bowl.

5. Carefully pour the egg into the center of the hole you cut out of the bread.

6. Place the cookie sheet into an oven pre-heated to 400 degrees and bake for 7-10 minutes. Serve while warm.

CONCOCTION TIPS & IDEAS:

• Use different shaped cookie cutters for various holidays and occasions.

BLT DIP

Grandma Thomas makes this tasty dip for almost every holiday celebration and the kids love it!

WHAT YOU WILL NEED:

1 round loaf of bread from the bakery (Sourdough is our favorite)

1 medium chopped tomato

1 cup mayonnaise

¾ cup sour cream

1 cup bacon pieces (either fresh cooked, precooked or real bacon pieces in a jar)

Dash of pepper to taste

HOW TO CONCOCT IT:

1. Cut the round top off of the loaf and tear the bread from the top into bite size pieces.

2. Hollow out the middle of the loaf to create a bowl, tearing the bread into bite size pieces.

3. Mix remaining ingredients together in a mixing bowl. Place the mixture in the refrigerator and chill for 4 hours before serving.

4. Place bread bowl on a platter and fill with dip. Arrange bread pieces around the bowl for dipping.

CONCOCTION TIPS & IDEAS:

• BLT Dip is also wonderful on crackers, toast or a slice of bread.

• Try using various different types of bread for your bowl including: Sourdough, French, Pumpernickel, etc.

STRAWBERRY BANANA SMOOTHIE

This is our favorite smoothie recipe of all time.

WHAT YOU WILL NEED:

1 cup orange juice or orange mango juice
½ cup vanilla yogurt or ice cream
1 banana
1½ cups frozen strawberries

HOW TO CONCOCT IT:

1. Place all of the ingredients into a blender.

2. Blend until smooth.

CONCOCTION TIPS & IDEAS:

• Experiment using various types of fruit juice, yogurt and ice cream.

GROOVY GRANOLA

The best granola recipe we have ever created.

WHAT YOU WILL NEED:

3 cups rolled oats

1 cup silvered almonds

1 cup cashews

¾ cup shredded sweet coconut

¼ cup dark brown sugar

¼ cup maple syrup

¼ cup vegetable oil

¾ tsp. salt

1 cup raisins

HOW TO CONCOCT IT:

1. Preheat oven to 250 degrees.

2. Mix all of the dry ingredients (except raisins) together in one bowl.

3. Mix all of the vegetable oil and syrup together in a separate bowl.

4. Combine the two mixtures together and pour evenly onto two different cookie sheets.

5. Cook in the oven for 1 hour and 15 minutes, occasionally stirring.

6. Pour into a large bowl, add raisins and mix.

CONCOCTION TIPS & IDEAS:

• Add ¼ up of mini chocolate chips along with the raisins to create Chocolate Groovy Granola.

FLAVORED ICE CUBES

Flavored Ice Cubes add pizzazz to ordinary drinks.

WHAT YOU WILL NEED:

2 cups lemonade
¼ cup finely chopped strawberries
1-2 Ice cube trays

HOW TO CONCOCT IT:

1. Mix lemonade and strawberries together in a small bowl.

2. Fill 1-2 ice cube trays with the mixture.

3. Place in the freezer until the ice cubes are frozen solid.

4. Add ice cubes to several glasses and fill with orange juice, ice tea, or soda water.

CONCOCTION TIPS & IDEAS:

• Mix various different types of finely chopped fruit and juice together to create other flavors of ice cubes.

FRUIT SALSA

Fruit Salsa is a refreshing treat that tastes great when paired with Cinnamon Tortillas

WHAT YOU WILL NEED:

1 pint chopped strawberries

Banana

1 chopped red delicious apple

1 peeled and chopped kiwi fruit

¼ cup lemon juice

¼ cup sugar

¼ tsp. ground nutmeg

½ tsp. cinnamon

HOW TO CONCOCT IT:

1. Mix all of the ingredients together in a large bowl.

2. Chill the mixture until ice cold.

3. Serve with Cinnamon Tortilla Crisps.

CONCOCTION TIPS & IDEAS:

• Combine different types of chopped fruit and juice together to create other flavors of Fruit Salsa.

CINNAMON CRUNCH TORTILLA CHIPS

These sweet cinnamon tortilla chips are wonderful when dipped into Fruit Salsas

WHAT YOU WILL NEED:

4 - 7 ½ inch round flour tortillas
¾ tsp. cinnamon
2 Tbs. sugar
Vegetable spray

HOW TO CONCOCT IT:

1. Spray both sides of the tortillas with vegetable spray.

2. Mix the sugar and cinnamon together.

3. Sprinkle the cinnamon and sugar mixture on each side of the tortillas.

4. Cut each tortilla into 8 pieces.

5. Place the tortilla pieces on a cookie sheet and bake at 350 degrees for 6-8 minutes or until lightly brown.

CONCOCTION TIPS & IDEAS:

• Serve Cinnamon Crunch Tortilla Chips as a tasty light dessert following any meal.

Measurement Conversion Chart

U.S.	METRIC
¼ teaspoon	1 ml
½ teaspoon	2 ml
1 teaspoon	5 ml
1 tablespoon	15 ml
¼ cup	50 ml
1/3 cup	75 ml
½ cup	125 ml
2/3 cup	150 ml
¾ cup	175 ml
1 cup	250 ml

Food Coloring Blending Chart

COLORS	FOOD COLORING
Teal	3 drops red + 2 drops green
Orange	3 drops yellow + 1 drop red
Purple	3 drops red + 2 drops blue
Light Green	3 drops green + 1 drop yellow
Dark Red	3 drops red + 1 drop blue
Gold	4 drops yellow + 1 drop red